W9-COV-235

AMAZING ILLUSIONS

How to Make the Impossible (Look) Possible!

BY TOM MASON AND DAN DANKO
WITH JEFF FREDRIKSEN,
PROFESSIONAL
MAGICIAN

SCHOLASTIC INC.

NEW YORK·TORONTO·LONDON·AUCKLAND
SYDNEY·MEXICO CITY·NEW DELHI
HONG KONG·BUENOS AIRES

ISBN 0-439-90709-8

Copyright © 2006 by Scholastic Inc.

Design by Michaela Zanzani, Aruna Goldstein, Julia Melillo

Photography by Rocco Melillo

12 11 10 9 8 7 6 5 4 3 2   7 8 9 0/0

Printed in the U.S.A.

First Scholastic printing, November 2006

Table of Contents

Doing the Impossible

What looks real but really isn't? That's an illusion for you! Magicians are experts at the art of illusion. They can make you believe what you see, even when you know it's impossible!

Pulling a rabbit out of a hat and sawing someone in half are classic examples of illusions. Harry Houdini used to walk through a brick wall. David Copperfield once walked through an even bigger one: the Great Wall of China! Magicians love to make the audience believe that solid objects might not be as solid as they seem to be. Magicians fool our senses. And that's what you'll be doing, too!

- Push a pencil through a quarter.

- Melt a penny through someone's hand.

- Make a vanished coin reappear inside sealed boxes.

These are just some of the illusions you're about to learn. By using the magic tricks from your kit and some everyday stuff from around the house (like quarters, newspapers, and drinking glasses), you'll do what the greatest magicians of all time have done. You'll ask one simple question: What is real and what is an illusion?

And then, after you've done the "impossible," don't tell 'em how you did the trick. Every magician knows to keep the magic of illusions top secret!

What's in Your Kit

THREE-HOLE COIN BOX

Stick three quarters inside this box. Then push a pencil through each one. Turn the page to get started!

MAGIC TOWER

This tower allows you to slide a solid cube straight through a magic wand. You'll learn this illusion on page 15.

NESTING COIN BOXES

After you make a coin disappear, it'll reappear inside these nesting boxes. Find out how on page 11.

SECRET COIN DISK

This trick disk lets you push a coin through a drinking glass. It'll be easy when you find out how to use the trapdoor on page 19.

CUPS AND BALLS

Can a ball move right through a cup? These can! Move yourself to page 22 to learn the secret.

THE TOP SECRET MAGIC WEB SITE

Check out the *Top Secret Magic* web site at www.scholastic.com/topsecretmagic for more magic tricks and tips. Just bring along this book's password: MindTrick

Pencil Pushing

PUSH THREE PENCILS THROUGH THREE COINS!

Push a pencil through a coin? It's easy with your Three-Hole Coin Box. It has a hidden tray that slides the coins out of the pencils' way and lets the pencils pass right through.

What You Need

From Your Kit:
* Three-Hole Coin Box

Plus:
* A piece of paper
* Scissors
* Three quarters
* Three sharpened pencils

PREPARE...

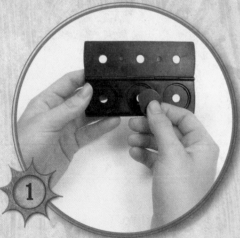

Open your Three-Hole Coin Box and find the key. It's that flat plastic thing with a little point on the end. The key unlocks a hidden tray inside the box.

To release the tray, push the pointed end of the key into the small rod that sticks out from the hinge on the left side of the Coin Box.

3

Tilt the Coin Box slightly downward and to the left; the tray should slide right out. Then slide the tray back to its starting position.

4

Next, cut a piece of paper so that it's about 1¼ inches wide and 6 inches long. It should be wide enough to fit inside the Coin Box and long enough to stick out on both sides by at least ¾ of an inch. The paper will hide the tray when it slides out of the box. The paper will also serve as evidence, but we'll get to that later!

5 Before you start the trick, make sure the Coin Box is unlocked. Then hide the key in your pocket or somewhere else handy.

"Pushing a solid object through another solid object? Science says it's impossible, but magic lets me do it anyway."

Use this patter, or conversation, when you perform the trick!

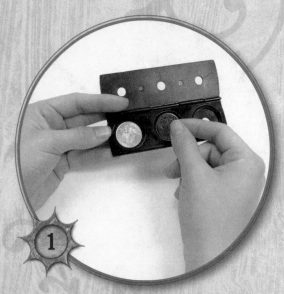

1

Show the Three-Hole Coin Box to the audience. Open the lid and let the audience watch as you place the three quarters inside, one at a time.

TRICK TIP:

Keep the box tilted slightly to the right as you put the quarters in so the tray doesn't slide open.

"I've got three quarters that are about as solid as you can get."

Place the piece of paper on top of the coins, then close the lid of the Coin Box. The paper should overhang both sides of the box evenly.

"And one piece of paper, which is also solid."

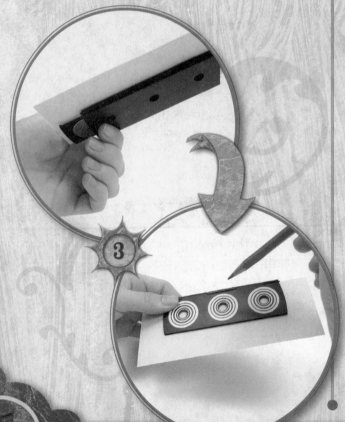

Turn the case slightly downward and to the left to let the tray fall out. It should be hidden by the overhanging paper. Then pick up one of the pencils with your free hand.

"The key to this trick is that I have to use my magician's breath."

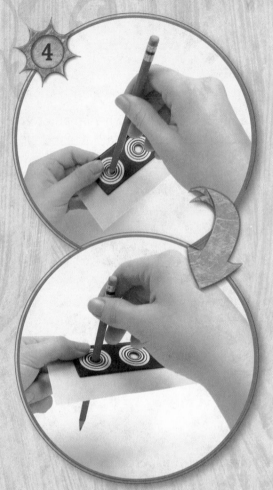

Blow on one of the pencils. Then push the pencil slowly and dramatically through the first quarter on the left. It should stick out from both sides of the Coin Box.

"This transfers the magic from me directly to the pencils..."

5

Repeat Step 4 with the second pencil and the second quarter.

"...so they can push their way..."

6

Repeat Step 4 one more time with the last pencil and the third quarter. All three pencils should be sticking out of both sides of the Coin Box.

"...through the solid quarters."

7

Reach around the front of the Coin Box with your right hand and slowly pull the pencils out, one at a time. As you pull out the last pencil, slide the tray closed with a finger on your left hand.

TRICK TIP:

Squeeze the box closed while you slide the tray in to keep the paper inside from shifting.

"Let's take a look at the evidence."

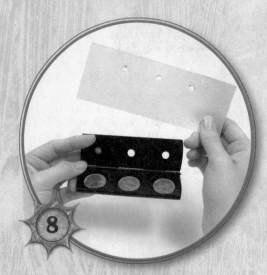

8

Open the lid of the Coin Box and hold up the paper to show the holes. One at a time, dump the coins on the table so the audience can see them.

"There are lots of liars in the world, but paper always tells the truth. The magic pencils went right through the quarters."

TRICK TIP:

When you're feeling confident about this trick, ask one of the audience members to step up and pull the pencils out.

As the audience leans forward to study the coins, casually relock the tray by pushing in the small rod that sticks out of the hinge on the right side.

"But the quarters are still in perfect shape. Maybe some of the pencil's magic rubbed off on them!"

Now, leave the lid of the Coin Box open and place it on the table. Let anybody from the audience pick up the Coin Box and look at it for as long as they want. Only you have the key, so your secret is safe!

PRACTICE!

Slide the tray out and back with one smooth move so the audience won't be able to see what you're doing.

MAGIC HISTORY

Most people make coins disappear by spending them. But magicians have been doing magic with coins for hundreds of years. In fact, the very first magic trick book, *The Discoverie of Witchcraft* by Reginald Scott (1584), has a few great coin tricks. Scott explains that coin tricks can be accomplished by using a coin made of two coins that have been sliced in half and stuck together back-to-back. That way depending on what side you're looking at, you see a different type of coin. All the magician has to do is secretly turn the coin over, and the audience will think that the first coin has left the magician's hand and another coin has taken its place!

My Coin Safe

MAKE A COIN APPEAR INSIDE FOUR SEALED BOXES!

Bonjour! This trick features a sleight-of-hand motion called the French Drop. (And that's not what happens when the Eiffel Tower falls over!) By misdirecting the audience's attention, you secretly move a quarter from your hand to your pocket.

What You Need

From Your Kit:
- ✻ Nesting Coin Boxes

Plus:
- ✻ A quarter
- ✻ A marker
- ✻ A volunteer

PREPARE...

Fit all the bottoms inside each other and do the same with the tops.

1

Tops

Bottoms

Split the nesting boxes into two groups—the tops and the bottoms (the bottoms have a lip around them, and the tops don't).

2

3

Place the bottoms in the bottom part of the black box holder and the tops in the top part, with the openings facing each other.

With your index finger and thumb, practice sliding the tops and bottoms together to create one box with the three other boxes hidden inside. You'll need to master this move before you start.

5 When you're ready, put the box holder in your right-hand pocket, arranged as shown in Step 3. You should be able to reach in and close it as shown in Step 4.

"Every now and then I get some extra money, like this quarter."

Display the quarter to the audience.

"So I don't lose it or get it confused with someone else's quarter, I like to mark it."

Pick a volunteer, give her the marker, and have her mark the quarter with an X on both sides. After that's done, hold the quarter between the thumb and index finger of your right hand.

"I want to keep my money in a safe place, but you can't really put a quarter in a bank. They'd laugh at me. I could put it in a piggy bank, but then somebody could grab the bank and run off with it."

3

Now it's time for your French Drop. To start, bring your left hand over like it's going to grab the quarter. Bring your thumb in front of the quarter and your fingers behind it.

"But I can't go around carrying my money in my hand all the time."

4

As your left fingers come behind, let the quarter fall from your fingertips into your right palm.

"I could easily drop my quarter or lose it."

5

Close your left hand, pretending that it has the quarter, and move it away to your left. The audience is watching your left hand closely. Now, while they're trying to figure out what's up with your left hand, drop your right hand casually at your side, holding the quarter in your right fingers. *Très bien* (good work)! You've done a French Drop!

"So the only thing I came up with was to hide the money."

6

Open up your left hand to the audience like you're going to reveal the quarter. Except...the quarter is gone!

"And I found the perfect place for it."

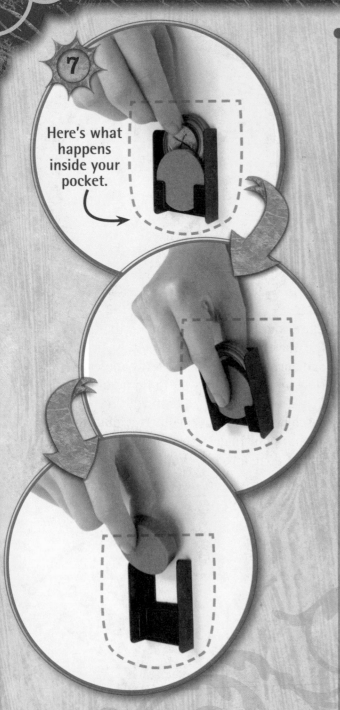

7 Here's what happens inside your pocket.

Casually reach into your pocket with your right hand. As you do this, place the quarter inside the secret nest of boxes. As soon as the quarter's in place, slide the two sets of boxes together. Remove all of the boxes as one unit from your pocket. But leave the box holder in your pocket.

TRICK TIP:

Perform this trick standing behind a table so that the audience can't see the outline of the slide in your pants pocket. Baggy pants help, too!

"It's safer than a bank and better than leaving it in my hand."

Remove the top from the outside box. Open the next one. Open the third. Open the fourth to reveal the marked quarter inside.

8

"Don't you agree?"

PRACTICE!

Practice the French Drop in front of a mirror. It's also important to get really slick at placing the quarter inside the boxes and sealing them up. This should be done in one smooth move. The more you fumble and fiddle, the more the audience will start to suspect!

The Magic Tower

SLIDE A CUBE THROUGH YOUR MAGIC WAND!

By now, you're probably starting to believe that is really is possible to push a solid object through another object. But your audience is always going to be amazed. Especially when a cube moves right through your magic wand!

What You Need

From Your Kit:
* Magic Tower

Plus:
* Magic wand or pencil

 PREPARE...

1. The magic tower is the long rectangular piece of cardboard. Gently push the edges toward each other so that you've got a long tube, and then stand it up on the table.

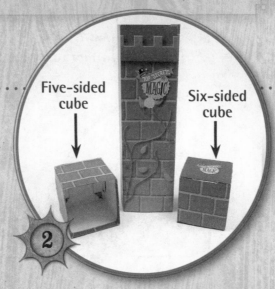

Five-sided cube

Six-sided cube

2. Assemble the two cubes by sticking all of the cardboard tabs into the little slits. We'll call the cube without a bottom the *five-sided cube*. We'll call the complete cube the *six-sided cube*.

15

Place the six-sided cube inside the five-sided cube. Then turn it over so the open end is down. Now it looks like you've just got one cube.

PERFORM!

"You know what I love? Ice cream. But I also love the story of King Arthur and the Knights of the Round Table and the famous wizard, Merlin."

Pick up the tower, and turn it toward the audience to show them that it's empty. Place it back on the table.

"Someday, I hope to build my own castle and use it as a magic school, so I can teach magic tricks."

Hold up the five-sided cube (with the six-sided one inside), squeezing it slightly so the cubes stay together.

"I'm going to have really tall towers in my castle, just like this one here...but I'm not going to have steps inside."

Drop the two-in-one cube down the top of the tower so that the open end of the five-sided cube goes in first.

"A magician doesn't need steps—I'll just float up and down inside the tower."

Squeeze the tower bottom gently with one hand to trap the five-sided cube inside. Then lift the tower to allow the six-sided cube to fall out.

Set the tower back down, next to the six-sided cube. Pick up the six-sided cube, and casually toss it in your hand so the audience sees that it's solid. Toss it to someone in the audience, and have them toss it back. Then, pick up the magic wand with your free hand.

"And, being a magician, I won't have to worry about crashing into anything inside the tower."

Slide the magic wand through the holes in the tower.

"I mean, suppose someone left their gigantic magic wand in the middle of the tower."

Drop the six-sided cube inside the tower.

"That's no problem at all; a good magician (like myself) will just float right through the wand and down to the bottom of the tower."

8 The six-sided cube will fall through the tower, but it'll stop when it gets to the wand. Now the trick really gets interesting!

Lift up the tower from the middle. This releases the five-sided cube. The audience will think it's the same cube that they saw you drop down the tower in Step 7. Put the tower away as quickly as possible so no one can see the real six-sided cube inside!

"See?"

PRACTICE!

Rehearse Step 4 by picking up the tower again and again, making sure that you keep the five-sided cube hidden inside as the six-sided cube falls out.

TRICK TIP:

Turn the tower so that one of the sides without the holes is facing the audience. That way, they can see both ends of the magic wand, but they can't look through the tower holes and see your cube!

18

The Coin Press

PUSH A COIN THROUGH A GLASS!

A drinking glass is solid as can be. Sounds like the perfect kind of object to pass a coin through! With your Secret Coin Disk, you'll be passing money through glasses with no problem.

What You Need

From Your Kit:
* Secret Coin Disk

Plus:
* Two quarters
* A handkerchief or scarf
* A clear plastic drinking glass

PREPARE...

2 Put one of the quarters inside the trap and close it up.

3 Make sure the open end of the glass fits just inside the edge of the blue disk or snugly around the outside of the disk.

1 Turn the blue disk upside down. A trapdoor will open up in the disk.

PERFORM!

"I have a fun trick with this drinking glass that always makes my mom nervous. No, she's not afraid I'll break the glass. She's worried that if I keep practicing my magic tricks, I'll never have time to clean my room."

1 Show the empty glass to the audience. Place it upside down on top of the blue disk, and hold up a quarter.

"I keep telling her to relax."

2

Place the quarter on top of the glass and cover the glass, the quarter, and the disk with the handkerchief. Then place the disk, glass, quarter, and handkerchief all in your open left palm.

"Even if I weren't practicing my magic, I still wouldn't clean my room!"

3 Press your palm down on the quarter as if you're trying to push it through the glass.

"But, back to the glass. I'm going to push a quarter right through it. With a little magical force...like so!"

4

Place your right palm over the quarter and the handkerchief. Hold the glass and disk between your two hands, and give it a shake.

This releases the quarter from the blue disk. The audience will hear it clink inside the glass.

Pull the handkerchief off the glass with your right hand, picking up the quarter with it. After you do that, immediately shove the handkerchief and the quarter into your pocket. *"And the quarter goes right through the glass without breaking it!"*

PRACTICE!

The key to this trick is hiding the quarter in Step 5. Practice grabbing the quarter with your thumb and hiding it with the handkerchief so the audience won't see it.

MAGIC HISTORY

Tony Slydini was a master of intricate pocket tricks that require practice in front of a mirror. Born in Argentina, Slydini moved to New York City in 1930, where he performed his miracles with cards and coins. Slydini was best known for crumpling a piece of paper into a ball and making it vanish right before a spectator's eyes. The secret? He was so close to the person's face that he simply tossed the ball over his or her head!

Lights! Camera! Drop! Vanish!

MAKE A BALL JUMP INTO AN UPSIDE-DOWN CUP!

Ever wonder how magicians make coins appear behind people's ears or balls appear under cups? It's all about *palming*—hiding an object in your hand. By hiding one ball under a cup before you begin this trick and then palming a second ball, you'll create the illusion that the ball has jumped from your hand to the cup.

What You Need

From Your Kit:
* One cup and two balls

PREPARE...

Drop a ball into a cup (you'll keep this a secret from your audience).

PERFORM!

"Did you ever hear the story of how Harry Houdini broke into a locked safe without opening the door? Well, I'm going to do the exact same trick... without the safe."

Show the audience the second ball and the cup. Make sure they can't see the first ball hidden in the cup!

"I've got this one ball. Let's call him Harry. And since I don't have a safe, this cup will have to do."

Flip the cup upside down onto the table. Since the cup has the secret ball inside, flip it quickly and carefully so the ball doesn't fly out.

"I'm going to ask little Harry here to pass through the solid cup and appear underneath. Sometimes Harry gets an attitude and doesn't want to do the trick, so no insults, please. He's very sensitive."

Stick your right fist on top of the cup and put "Harry" on top of your fist.

"Now, I'll just open my fist and let the ball fall onto the cup."

This step is called the *drop vanish*. Loosen the fingers of your right hand so the ball falls into, but not *through*, your fist. Don't let the ball fall onto the cup. Instead, let it rest near your ring finger. Pull your hand away from the cup, revealing that there is no ball on top. You've just done a drop vanish!

"So I'll take this ball and...hey! Where'd it go?"

Keeping the ball palmed in your right hand, lift the cup with your index finger and thumb, revealing the second ball (which has been hanging out under the cup all along).

"Ah! There he is! He broke right into the cup, just like Harry Houdini!"

PRACTICE!

The drop vanish can be tricky, so don't be discouraged! You want the motions to be as natural as possible to fool the audience.

Take Me Out to the Ball Game

FORCE BALLS THROUGH MULTIPLE CUPS!

You just made a ball pass through a cup in the last trick. In this trick, you'll really dazzle your audience by doing it again and again!

What You Need

From Your Kit:
- ✳ Three cups, four balls

Plus:
- ✳ Magic wand or pencil (optional)

PREPARE...

1 Place the blue cup inside the yellow cup, mouth up.

2 Drop one of the balls inside the blue cup.

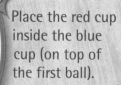

3 Place the red cup inside the blue cup (on top of the first ball).

Now, drop the three remaining balls inside the red cup.

PERFORM!

"This magic trick is as old as the ancient Egyptians, but it still works today."

Grab the three cups as one and pour out the three balls from the red cup onto the table.

"When it was first done, they used stone balls and bowls. Now it's more modern: I've got these plastic cups..."

Line up the three balls in a row on the table. Press on them with your fingers to show the audience that they are soft and fuzzy.

"...and there's nothing more modern than these three fuzzy little balls."

Make sure this ball stays hidden from your audience.

Remove the red cup and turn it upside down behind the ball on your left.

4

Remove the blue cup and turn it upside down behind the middle ball. Do this quickly so the ball hidden inside doesn't fall out and roll away.

TRICK TIP:

When turning the cups over, hold them near the mouth of the cup. That makes it easier to keep the hidden ball inside.

Turn over the yellow cup behind the ball on the right.

"Even though they are fuzzy and little..."

5

6

Pick up the ball in front of the blue cup and place it on top of the blue cup.

"...they pack a lot of power."

7

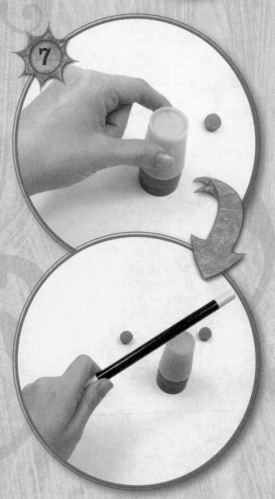

Keeping the ball on top of the blue cup, put the red cup and then the yellow cup upside down over the blue cup. If you want, tap the top of the yellow cup with your magic wand or pencil.

"When you combine their fuzzy ball power with the power of the magic wand..."

8

Lift the three cups as one and set them down mouth up, revealing one fuzzy ball underneath.

"...the fuzzy ball will blast its way through one of the cups."

There are 2 balls in here now.

9

Line up the three balls again. Now, put the blue cup behind the right ball. Take the red cup (the one that still has the hidden ball left over from the previous trick), and place it *over* the middle ball. Then put the yellow cup behind the ball on the left.

"Okay, so that works with one ball, but can I get a second fuzzy ball to go through the cup and join the first one?"

10

Lift up the ball in front of the yellow cup and place it on top of the red cup.

"Let's see."

11

Place the blue cup upside down over the red cup. Then place the yellow cup upside down over the blue cup. If you want, tap the yellow cup twice with the magic wand.

"I may have to use the power of the magic wand twice this time."

Lift up the three cups as one and set them down mouth up. Two balls will appear underneath.

"Let's try this one more time—but let's make it harder."

There are 3 balls total now.

Remove the red cup from the stack and place it on the left. Remove the blue cup and put it over the two balls grouped in the middle (making sure not to let anyone see the ball inside). Then place the yellow cup behind the remaining ball.

"Can I get the third ball to pass through not one but two cups and join the first two balls?"

Place the red cup upside down over the blue cup. Pick up the right ball, and place it on the red cup. Pick up the yellow cup, and turn it upside down over the other two cups. If you want, tap the yellow cup three times with the magic wand.

Lift up the three cups together. Three balls will remain on the table.

"And sure enough, a fuzzy ball can pass through two cups!"

MAGIC HISTORY

The cups and balls trick is one of the classic tricks by which a true magician's talent is judged. And when we say classic, we mean that this is a really, really old trick. The ancient Egyptians used to have three little chicks appear under the cups for a grand finale! The undisputed twentieth-century master of the cups and balls was the late Canadian magician Dai Vernon. He was the wise old Merlin of magic. Other magicians would call him "the Professor" and come from all over the world to study the art with him in his castle— the Magic Castle in Hollywood, CA. His secret? "Practice, practice, practice."

The Rubber Band Jump

MAKE A RUBBER BAND SWITCH FINGERS!

This is an example of a trick that does itself. Just put the rubber band in the right place, and you can make it jump from your first two fingers to your second two like magic!

What You Need

✷ Two rubber bands of different colors

 PERFORM!

"A rubber band is good for a lot of things. Wrap it around newspapers, shoot it in the air, or use it to tie up packages. But all that stuff's boring. Because I'm a magician, I can make a rubber band jump right through my fingers."

1

Let the audience watch as you loop a rubber band around the index and middle finger of your left hand.

"Like this regular rubber band here. It's on my two fingers."

Curl your fingertips away from the audience, like you're making a fist. As you do this, stretch the rubber band out with your right hand and let it rest against the fingernails of your four left fingers.

"But not for very long."

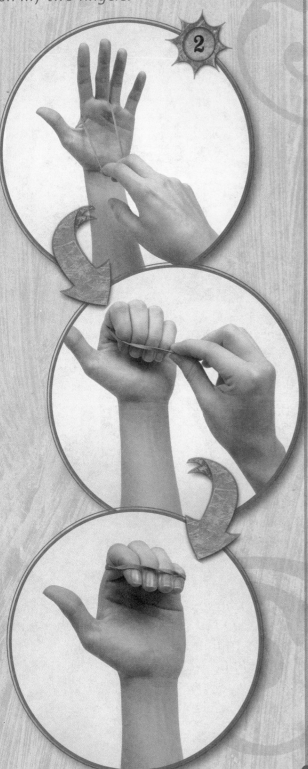

Uncurl your fingers. As you do, the rubber band will automatically jump to your ring and little fingers.

"Cool, huh? Who knew rubber bands were such great escape artists? But let's see just how talented that rubber band is. And for that, I need a second rubber band."

"This second rubber band will go over all my fingers to try to stop my first rubber band from jumping."

Set up the first rubber band like you did in Step 1. Then loop the second rubber band around your little finger. Twist it once, then loop it over your ring finger. Twist it once more and loop it over your middle finger, and twist it one last time and loop it over your index finger.

Repeat Step 2.

"Or will it?"

Uncurl your fingers. The rubber band jumps to your other fingers, just like it did before.

"Score: Rubber bands 2, Magician 0. I guess when a rubber band wants to jump, there's nothing you can do to stop it."

Paper Clipped

MAGICALLY LINK
TOGETHER TWO PAPER CLIPS!

If you think of paper clips as just boring school supplies, think again. Here's a cool trick that links them together, using only a dollar bill. The folds of the dollar automatically push apart the sides of the paper clips, then link them together as you pull at the ends of the bill.

What You Need

* Two big paper clips
* A dollar bill
* A rubber band

 ## PERFORM!

"I love going down to the magic store and learning all the new tricks. They have this really cool one called the Chinese Linking Rings where you can hook solid rings together to make a chain. I wanted to get it, but I'd spent all my money on video games and only had this dollar left over."

Fold a dollar bill into thirds in the shape of a Z.

"But I came up with my own version of that trick, using my leftover dollar."

1

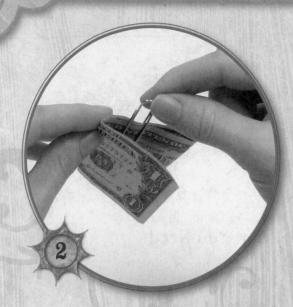

Place one paperclip on the left side, clipping the back and middle sections of the dollar.

"I just fold the dollar like this and clip it with these regular paper clips."

Place the second paper clip on the right side, clipping the middle and front sections of the dollar.

"And when I pull the dollar apart..."

Quickly pull the ends of the dollar bill apart. The paper clips will fly into the air. When they land, they'll be hooked together.

"Cool, huh? But I didn't want paper clips flying all over the house and getting lost. So I came up with a variation."

5

6

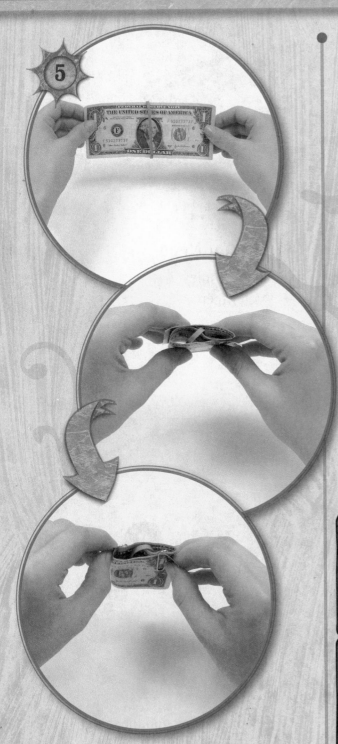

Now, pull the ends of the bill apart quickly. The paper clips are linked together and attached to the rubber band!

"Now the paper clips are still linked together, but they're also attached to the rubber band so they can't get away!"

Loop a rubber band once around the middle of the bill. Now, fold the bill, and clip it exactly as you did in Steps 2 and 3. Make sure the rubber band ends up in the middle of the folds, between the two paper clips.

"I added a rubber band."

MAGIC HISTORY

PAPER CLIPPED is very similar to the famous Chinese Linking Rings. No one knows when it was first performed in China, but the first performance in Europe was by a nineteenth-century Frenchman known only as Philippe. Many methods have been used to link and unlink what appear to be solid rings of steel. One simple method is to simply switch two unlinked rings for two linked ones when the audience is momentarily distracted.

Penniless

PASS A PENNY
THROUGH SOMEONE'S HAND!

If your audience hears seven pennies fall into a volunteer's hand one by one, they'll believe seven pennies are really there. But you'll only drop in six—which lets you create the illusion that you've passed the seventh penny right through your volunteer's hand.

What You Need

❋ Seven pennies
❋ A volunteer

 **PERFORM!**

"To ordinary humans, pennies are totally boring. But to magicians like me—they're totally boring, too! I still keep 'em, though, because I can still use them for magic. One thing I can do with pennies is make them pass through human skin."

1

Place the seven pennies on the table. Find a volunteer, and ask her to step right up.

"I've got seven pennies here, and I want you to pick them up off the table and then drop them in my hand one at a time. Count them out loud as you do it, okay?"

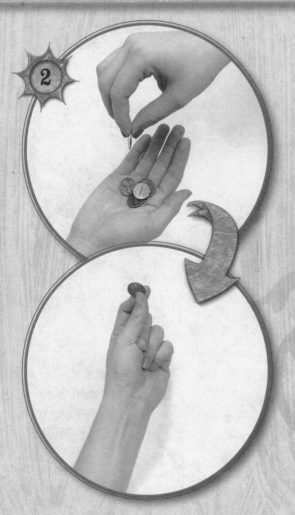

2

Hold out your right hand, and let her count out the pennies. When she's finished, pick up one penny with your left hand.

"Now don't be scared, but I can make this penny pass through your hand."

3

Still holding that penny in your left hand, place the other six pennies, one at a time, from your right hand to the right hand of your

volunteer, and count them as you do it. Clink the pennies against each other as you place them. (The clinking sound helps reinforce the count in everyone's mind.)

"One, two, three, four, five..."

4

On the sixth penny, clink it against the others, say "six" out loud, but keep it in your fingers. *"...six..."*

5

Reach over with your left hand and place the seventh penny on top of the other five pennies in your volunteer's right hand.

"...and seven. All seven pennies are in your hand."

6

Have your volunteer close her hand into a fist and put your right hand (the one holding and hiding the sixth penny) under her fist.

"Now I'm going to make that penny pass through your skin, your bone, your blood vessels, and your tendons."

7

Tap the top of her hand with your left hand. *"And away it goes!"*

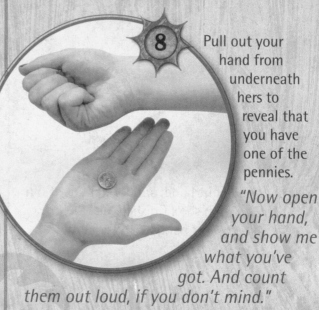

8 Pull out your hand from underneath hers to reveal that you have one of the pennies.

"Now open your hand, and show me what you've got. And count them out loud, if you don't mind."

9 Your volunteer will count out six pennies, as if the seventh one really did pass through.

PRACTICE!

Practice hiding the sixth penny as you clink it against the others in Step 4

Saw the Straw

CUT A DRINKING STRAW IN HALF WITHOUT CUTTING THE STRING INSIDE!

Straws are great for slurping up your favorite drink, but you can also use them for magic when you're done. Using a secret slit in the straw, a pair of scissors can cut through the straw and above the string. The straw gets snipped in two pieces, and the string remains uncut!

What You Need

✶ String
✶ A drinking straw
✶ Scissors

PREPARE...

1

Cut the piece of string about 4 inches longer than the straw.

2

Pinch the straw in the middle and cut a tiny snip in the straw. Then insert your scissors into that snip and cut a small slit lengthwise along the straw.

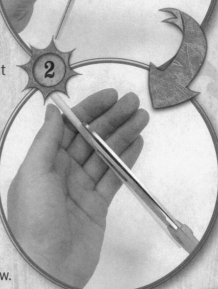

PERFORM!

"One of magic's oldest tricks is sawing someone in half. A person is placed in a box and cut into two pieces, but afterward, the person's still whole. Well, none of my friends wanted to be cut in two, but not to worry, I can use a substitute."

3

Thread the string through the straw so that it dangles evenly out of both ends.

"I'll place my substitute person inside the box. And now for the sawing-in-half part!"

1

Pick up the piece of string from the table.

"Here is my substitute. He's a little on the boring side, but hey, you can't have everything."

2

Pick up the straw with your other hand and hold it with the slit facing you so that the audience can't see it.

"And here is the box."

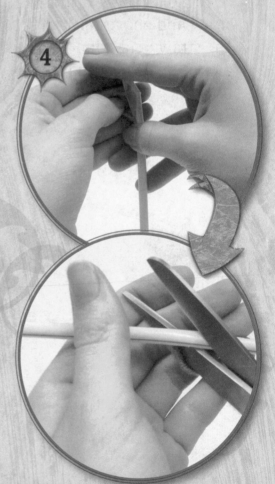

4

Bend the straw and quickly pull the string toward you through the slit. Insert the scissors between the string and the straw, keeping your palm around the straw to cover up what you're doing. Then cut through the straw.

"Ouch. That's got to hurt...except for one thing..."

5

Slide apart the two pieces of the straw—the string is uncut!

"My substitute person is still in one piece!"

MAGIC HISTORY

In 1920, the English magician P. T. Selbit invented the world's most popular trick, sawing a woman in half. It was an immediate sensation. In Selbit's original version, the woman stepped into a long box and had her feet and head strapped down. When the lid was closed and she was completely out of view, she would secretly slip her feet out of the straps and curl up in a ball as the saw cut the box into two separate halves. Over the years many improvements have been made to this illusion. The most important is keeping the woman's head and feet in full view at all times. Today in Las Vegas, a number of magicians perform a version of this illusion in which there is no box. The magician is strapped to a table, and the audience can see a huge buzz saw cut right through the magician's middle, leaving him unharmed!

Smashing Glass

SMACK A GLASS THROUGH A TABLE!

If you want a trick that really makes the audience jump, this is it. It's great sleight-of-hand magic that catches the audience completely by surprise. A paper "mold" of a cup makes the audience think the cup is still on the table. After you smash the paper, they're shocked when you pull out the real cup from under the table!

What You Need

* A plastic or foam cup
* A sheet of newspaper
* A quarter
* A table
* A magic wand or pencil

 **PERFORM!**

"I've got a normal cup, a sheet of newspaper, and my lucky quarter."

Hold up the cup and set it on the table upside down.

"Now, I'm going to make this quarter go right through the table! But first, I've gotta get the cup ready. First I cover the cup..."

Cover the cup with the newspaper and mold it with your hand until it's in the shape of the cup. The newspaper should completely cover the cup. Place the quarter on the table, about a foot from the edge.

Place the covered cup over the coin. Tap the top of the cup three times.

"Now, I place the covered cup over my quarter for just a quick second... and the quarter should be..."

Lift up the cup. Surprise! The coin is still there. Look disappointed, then act like you just remembered something.

"Shoot! I must have...of course! I forgot the magic wand!"

Put the covered cup back over the quarter. Tap the top three times with your magic wand or a pencil.

"Abracadabra! And the quarter is..."

Lift up the covered cup and bring it toward you, over your lap. Loosen your grip slightly and let the cup fall into your lap while you hold the newspaper. The newspaper should keep the same shape, as if the cup was still there. Keep looking at the quarter, which is still on the table, as if you didn't expect it to be there.

"All right, let's try this one more time."

PRACTICE!

Work on your cup-dropping technique—practice letting the cup fall into your lap as you hold onto the newspaper mold, all without looking at that hand.

Place the paper on top of the quarter again. Then, quickly slam your left hand on top of the paper like you just crushed the cup!

8

Reach under the table with your right hand, pull out the cup, and put it back on the table.

"Oh, that's right. This is a trick that makes the cup go through the table! I'll save the coin for next time."

TRICK TIP:

If you're having trouble getting the newspaper to take the shape of the cup, try this trick with alumium foil— it's easier to mold and holds its shape better.

MAGIC HISTORY

Max Malini was a master of tricks with drinking glasses. Born in Ostrov, Poland, in 1873, he grew up in New York City and lived in Chicago when not performing for kings, queens, and presidents. He'd place a coin on a restaurant table and cover it with his hat. "Heads or tails?" he'd ask. After he had his answer, he'd lift his hat to reveal a full glass of liquid. How did he do it? Misdirection. Malini was an expert at it!

The Paper Door

WALK THROUGH A PIECE OF PAPER!

This is a goofy trick, but it's really fun. By cutting a piece of paper in just the right places, you create a giant strip that's big enough to walk through.

What You Need

* A piece of letter-size paper
* Scissors

PERFORM!

"Paper has a lot of magic properties, but it takes a real magician to be able to bring them out."

1 Hold up the piece of paper so that the audience can see that there's nothing tricky about it. Let them touch it or hold it themselves if you want.

"This piece of paper, for example, is really a door that I can walk right through."

2 Fold the paper in half lengthwise.

"The secret to walking through a piece of paper is finding the hidden door. The guy who invented paper was pretty tricky."

3 Cut in from the fold almost to the edge, several times. Each cut should be about 2 inches from the previous cut.

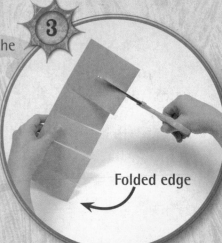

Folded edge

"But if you know what you're doing and cut along the secret passageway..."

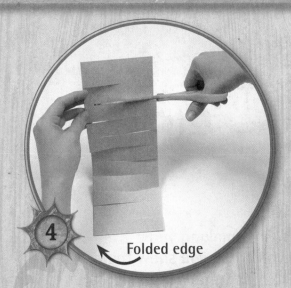

4

Folded edge

Turn the paper around so that it's facing the opposite direction. Now cut between the slits you've made, starting from the unfolded edges and cutting almost to the folded edge.

"...and then you cut some more..."

5

Turn the paper around again so that it's in the position it was in Step 2. Cut along the fold between the first cut and the last one. Make sure not to cut the fold at the very top and bottom of the paper.

"...very quickly, you can find the door..."

6

Now open up the paper, and show the hole to the audience.

"...and walk right through it!"

TRICK TIP:

The closer together you make your cuts in Step 3, the bigger your paper "door" will be.

Can You Believe It?

It's no illusion. You're now a master at making your audience see it and believe it—even when you show them something totally impossible, like a ball that's just passed through a solid plastic cup!

You've forced a pencil through a quarter, made a rubber band jump around on your hand, and smacked a cup through your dining room table—without making your mom mad. Your fingers are probably tired (and probably, so are the quarters, the rubber band, and the cup), but that might be an illusion, too.

While your audience is still scratching their heads trying to figure out what's real and what isn't, you should be getting ready for your next *Top Secret Magic* book. Stay tuned for more tricks and trickery, more tips, more practice, and of course, more magic!